Words for Women
Lori Heninger

QUILLKEEPERS PRESS

Table of Contents

Praise for
Words for Women

Words for Women takes the reader on a wild ride from the language of derision to the messages that shout, "I will not be denied!" Required reading for anyone bold enough to look themselves in the mirror—and see who's really there.

—Gay Norton Edelman, writing coach, spiritual life coach

Harpy, Nag, Witch, Whore; harsh words for women that chafe, prickle and judge ; Darling, Eve,Housewife, Mamma; words that may elevate women well beyond livable altitudes. Lori Heninger's Words for Women makes bold use of these many labels, an itemized Sears catalog of WOMEN defined by a single word. Heninger's progression of poems reveal these words aimed at women are also for them to own, embrace or reject, reconfigure and master. The poems in Words for Women, courageously with humor, fury and pathos, push past an imposed monotone singularity to command a chromatic wonder of possibility well beyond superficial designations.

— Dr. Lou Storey

For every woman who rises again.

Harpy

"Hey! I got a job fa da three a yas"
thundered Zeus to the Gorgons; "since
nobody wants youse—the stink is enough
to drop the Minotaur—and since youse
is *the hounds of Zeus*, my *made* ladies,

there's dis guy, Phineus of Thrace, I gave
him a gift and he sang like a canary. Now
I axe you, is dat any way ta treat a god?"

"It's an easy one;
I already took his eyes,
all youse gotta do is shit
every day all over da buffet I lays out.
Let him smell it first, know what he's missin,

then the tree a yas take whatcha want,
work up a good dump,
bury all the rest. Kapish?"

Nag

She's at it again, the wife,
it's my way of getting
back at her for all the times
I wanted sex and she rolled over, looking too good
or too bad at neighbors' parties,
for making me go to those parties.

Sometimes I just forget
to do my chores, the stuff
outside the inside of the house,
(other than the inside of the garage)
my domain, the land of grass blades
and power washers, of metal and sharp edges.

I'm stuck. The body double,
I just want to tinker and watch the games,
not pick up my dirty clothes every day,
keep things afloat (intentional oversight,
she works too), maybe that's the rub:

She doesn't need me, not really,

could do it herself, or hire someone.

Sometimes I think all of this,

all of me, is a drag on her speed.

So I forget, or on purpose don't finish the job,

adding to the ballast to slow her down.

Tart

Upon my cart

I have some tarts

cherry-filled and toothsome,

just pick one up

they're cheap enough,

and home with you they'll come.

I see you, John,

pay or walk on.

     I've little time for talk,

it's business, dear,

if that's not clear,

     you're dumber than I thought.

Doll I

Hey Doll!
you in your heels and straight stocking seams
going wherever dolls go,
wherever broads go
(nowhere narrow);
What a tomata! all curves
and juicy, a little green hat,
some salt and I'd eatcha up!

It's just a comp-li-ment—a way
to show my appreciation for ya,
what god put onto this earth for me to hold.

Baby if I make you blush, warm
around the neck and cheeks, well
I've done my job, shown you
whose boss, cause in a fistfight
outside the bar, you'd lose those pearly whites.

Wait, men don't hit women,
wait   wait

You walk on, I won, the words,
you smile. Or frown. That's
all you got. It's all I'll let you have.

Doll II

When my first husband was young
his father said no to GI Joes:
they were dolls. Boys didn't play
with dolls.

His friend across the street
had GI Joes, they played;
one day my ex pulled off
their GI heads, then in a row,

hung them by their necks
from the sole front-yard tree.

Battle Axe

Uncle Fred owned a chicken farm
in New Jersey, his wife, my mother's sister,
Myrtle. By the time I knew them, the chickens
were gone, they lived in a small, one-story house,
road ending at reedy, cattailed wetlands,
train tracks at the bottom of a gully
beyond the chain-link boundary of their backyard.

Family parties, when their turn,
held on a jalousie -windowed back porch;

> (I, invited into the room
> of my wheelchair-bound cousin
> for Polaroids; twenty-five years
> older than my eleven
> had me sit on a wood chair,
> told me to pull my skirt "higher, no *higher*"
> I could not have made the connection
> between my thighs and his cock)

cement, floored, Fred drank Brioschi,

belched; at the table

his mother-in-law, Pearl,

called her *old Battle-axe*

his joke, she laughed

/six daughters, widow,

psychosis, no permanent home/

a spot-lit minute, recognition

of her place at the table.

Cow

She's a cow she's a sow she's a haus   frau
She's a bag she's a hag she's a wet   rag
She's a bore she's a whore she's an open   sore
Flat as a board, oh my lord

    I'll fuck her anyway.

Darling

I

Wendy, my darling you were typecast

long ago as mother, mother to flying boys

whose histories of mischief and war

thrust you into situations not of your making:

tied to a mast, hook-handed pirates

closing in; boys (not *all* boys)

act before they think, little plan;

you with your assigned role

and craving to fly, followed.

II

Darling, how I love you

Darling, you are so darling

Darling, you are a tiny light

Tender and coy, my darling

My tiny, glittering darling

III

Angel, baby, treasure, sugar,

pet, sweetie

dear, dearie, dearest

apple of my eye, honeybunch

one and only, precious

light of my life, darling.

IV

A darling is about as deep

as the movie screen on which she's projected.

V

You. I stand, look down,

your face frozen lacks light,

my grief, my grief,

my darling.

Eve

Adam, as usual parking the car in the lot;

Eve, ever patient waits for him to find

the right space, not too close to

neighboring vehicles, doesn't want the paint scratched,

not near the curb don't ding the wheels

and, to be fair,

makes for getting out of a low-slung car simpler.

She, a lifetime of driving, having to take the wheel,

wrest it from the hand of god like she did

the apple from the tree, she could not bear,

for another second, infinity of the son

walking that garden

naming every fucking thing,

dominion over all,

cock and balls swinging as he strode;

clueless about everything. Everything

god told him he was, Eve knew he was not,

the apple, the only way. She knew,

reduced to helpmate, used sex,

plunked that apple between her thighs and led his head,

his lips, right to the red—tongue-flick, then his teeth:

he bit. He swallowed.

The bible lied: change was not immediate;

Eve knew the truth god hid, god would pull

every string to keep his boy in charge,

jerk him like a puppet unaware of its binds

until small shoots, branches, apple blossoms

bloomed and he

(the man),

saw that what he believed to be his

will was not his at all.

Eve closed the car door,

handed him a pair of scissors, said,

Let's cut those cords.

Housewife

That's all for me: mid-century modern;
low-backed black nubbly-fabricked couches
and low-slung sleek blonde tables. I cleaned
them, my job: keep the house spotless,
gold carved wall to wall, clay lamps
inscribed with squares of turquoise and orange,
a green glass ashtray, all mine
to keep dustless; the marks that couch left
on the backs of my thighs,
red stripes and indents disappeared
until I sat down again.

Sorceress

I want to set you straight:
sorceresses and witches, we're sisters,
but fate dealt witches
the ugly card, that's just how the deal went.

Sorceresses: runway models
of the supernatural set, strutting
and striding, all the spells and all the sex
in this curved, nipply, velvet-draped package.

Who could blame us if, like
the long, lean praying mantis,
we take an after-sex snack,
the heads of our couplers?

So, *don't*. *Don't* blame us
for what we are, how we came
into the world, for *your* inability
to distinguish hearts from clubs.

Witch

What can I tell you about us that you haven't already
heard over and over from the time you were a small
child, we cast spells and sprout hairy warts, are ugly and
eat small children, responsible for plagues and floods,
earthquakes and crop failures, your husband's
promiscuity, death of the neighbor's cat; we cast the evil
eye, speak with the dead and dance, naked, around
bonfires with Beelzebub and his buds

or

that we, all of *us* are daughters of earth, Mother Gaia;
wise, knowledge-seeking, remembering how a particular
plant, distilled, impacts symptoms of gout, or that our
monthly bleeding and ability
to produce children
create life
sets us apart,
incomprehensible, miraculous.

Sorry to have gone on so long, once I get started it's
hard to stop. Always the same shit with different labels:

whore/madonna

destroyer/healer

man eater/pie baker

All of it true and none of it; really, we are just like you:
flawed, gifted, prescient, clumsy. The sorceresses will
tell you lies about us (they *never* seek the facts); it's what
they do; not name-calling, just true; we understand too
well their need to be seen. The rest of us take the train
to work, sing in the shower, masturbate, wash some
dishes, cut the grass, sweat, sleep, dream.

Bitch

The edge of her rage   lies at the soft inside
of a bitten lip, between teeth and sweet
air   /all of the world   ;
lips, little exists except a line,
lip line, red,   red
in a dark space, a fleshy place
light rarely reaches, barely touches

Orb spider spins a silky threaded web,
secures a seal, sound, ensuring
it stalls inside, oh spider now   she knows why
you surface in nightmares,   symbol of all the flies
she's forced to catch: lips fixed
by sticky threads and flies

No surprise   she *rages*,
the line—a fast-moving river that:

cannot be crossed, cannot be crossed, cannot be crossed
        cannot be crossed cannot be crossed

Cassandra

Cassandra, after a time
began talking quietly to herself;
full sentences, not quite mumbling
coming events no one believed
but she knew,
she *knew*
came to pass, were true;

in her light gown, knees
atop the fecund earth
head bowed, lips
directed her words,
dropped seeds
toward finger-poked holes.

Cassandra, in her wild mind
knew the future crops she sowed:
a moon landing
a round earth
climate change
a woman's body is her own.

Poison Ivy

Did you know that ivy roots,
when pulled up, those tough mothers,
separate from the main runner giving the vine
a better chance of remaining buried?

Foiling weeders, that's the ruse,
it's life and life and life and life
below the dark earth.

Drama Queen

It's a big-screen, the leading lady and man silvered
black and white, it's the olden days but with sound;
few complexities or the mundane, no
changing diapers, no
driving to football practice or swim meets;

it's all evening gowns, waists and tiaras, cigarette holders
and well-cut suits hanging on broad shoulders, feathered
nightgowns could make a person sneeze in their sleep;

it's martinis in small glasses served from cocktail carts
strategically placed to keep the actors in frame.

Becoming in a small apartment in an unglamorous city,
poor, a bicycle with one pedal shared, one girl
pumped, one girl rode the handlebars knowing what they,
two, paid to see would never be theirs; perhaps the
longing and the romance were reason enough.

Mom

Yesterday staring into the barrel
of a portable rented cement mixer, a quarter full,
concrete and water, rolling, combining
inside the turning tub;
I've thought this before, how
it's like making a cake and, if you're stacking
bricks, spreading the gritty
ooze is the same as icing a layer;

the motions, the measuring, the mixing
so similar; not quite exact
one to the other, close enough.

Medusa

This afternoon, I sanded a staircase corner
chewed by the previous homeowner's dogs;
they were old and anxious,
they were *dogs*.

I love creating
order with tools in my hands,
the kinds of projects relegated,
in my small suburban space of growing up,
to men. I don't want
to do it all the time (like for a living),

but don't tell me to be the girl,
because I won't have it.

We are so many things.

Yesterday I painted the deck, well, part of the deck;
my sweat-soaked shirt stuck to my chest and back,
a dark line between
my shoulder blades
another outlining

my breasts,
short black sleeves wet from wiping
my forehead, my eyes.

Steam rose from the paint,
slick roller spreading sealer
atop the dry scarred boards power-washed
(by me) last week;
I will not stop till it is done.

I will not lay down these tools:
I hold my hammers and files, my paint trays
and sandpapers, my pickaxe, shovel and pliers,
these two lovely arms and two lovely hands
these fat-wrapped thighs and clicking, cracking brain,

this body full of muscle and lust; never, *never*
tell me who I am: I will outwit you
at each stone; outrun you in every trial,
then turn to let you see, in blind-you brilliance,
all of what I am.

Whore

It's not the same for all of us, I know, but this is the
body I wore into the world and, with the electrical
impulses jumping synapses in my brain, it's mine to use

as I want

for what they want; supply and demand, basic
capitalism, I've got it you crave it, I own it you pay for
those small pink holes, these tits that came with the XX
when I slid out of the birth canal;
simple metrics, all business and no shame;
if you want to believe it's more than that,
you're dumber than I thought.

Siren

I

We, the keepers of tones hold tight
to the ancient forms, recall notes from before
you were upright, bowls full of sounds

brought down; we collect songs spun
in a moon's crater, from the rotating arms
of the Milky Way, from the first harmonics of creation:

a tone made us all, summoned the stuff,
changed it via vibration, sang it into being

II

It's exhausting having to fight the lie,
the untruth of what you're told you are.

It's easier to deny, try to figure out a way
around;

then they call you *manipulative,*
a flesh-eater, as if

all of this was not, on their part,
projections of desire and lack of control
and mostly, fear. *We,*
cisterns for the fundamental resonance,
have no interest in men, or women.

Our commission is to sing.

Sailors classified us mantic; my sisters and I
had to look it up
here on the quiet island *(Surprise!)*
we have phones and broadband:

>first we were human woman heads
>stuck on the bodies of birds;
>it confused us,
>the way their mouths formed words

about our appearance: humiliated,

we raged, three minds as one,

finished each others' sentences,

decided then to end it; to end the passing;

rage became art, elemental anger, sung,

roiled the water;

they steered themselves

onto sharp stone points

and tore their bodies apart,

we left their flesh to rot:

we eat *fish*.

Centuries then, in calm seas we paddled

to wood water swollen sides of boats

to try conversation, negotiation,

show them they were

mislead, wrong about so much,

offered our wisdom

in exchange for truth-telling;

all sound fell into the sea and

drown, they sailed on,

crafted us mermaids
(because we could swim)

firm breasts and big nipples, flat stomachs and
flowing hair, glinting, winking fins,
fish tails and scales, nothing like us,
retreated to our island's cold caves
and stayed, not even pinochle
or a good dirge moved us.

Next early Christians passed;
set us back to women and birds
and the additional condition: virgins
with beauty *that deprives men of reason*
as if we had any spoon in the swirl
of our DNA, of our assigned role;

decided we'd project—but not accept—
what they believed and didn't question:
a Trojan Horse, didn't they learn
some things seem to be surrender
when day to day they are the core
of survival and victory.

Spinster I

Darkness of her hair contrasts with white wool
spinning, spinning on her worn wheel; floss into yarn,
washed then dyed, woven then cut. Sewn then worn,
worn out, patched, finally snipped for rags or quilts;

she knows the tale, told every day by her work, creation
and use, use and discard;

at twenty-three too old for marrying; relieved, she's
seen a sister paling, continuing to bleed after the baby's
head crowned, pile of bloody cloths tossed aside the
bed's edge, she collected all in a basket stained, saw red
wash water as they soaked;

better to sit and spin, watch and breathe, walk and nod.

Spinster II

As small as 50 years ago, my main goal was: have a

boylove, a committed relationship, a wedding;

few images of what I could hold (it all seemed so hard)

prepared me for that narrow track, less curious about

the world outside my stable, how I was groomed. That

was my plan. My lead rope, my grounding.

Ground   ing

ground down to the basics, the mash and hay suburban

girls understood (with a bucket of post-60s revolution)

which was:

> TNT in dirt just below the track,
>
> exploding if a random match,
>
> carelessly tossed from the hand that lit a
>
> cigarette happened to land in the right space, the
>
> correct place; I knew nothing when earth
>
> cracked and clods flew, striking me, didn't know
>
> what to do, looked into the hole unaware as a
>
> brood mare, forgot the plan, ran.

Spinster III

This your old woman talking; it's not like it used to be,

there's less chance of you ending up bitter and alone

than bitter married, having to trade off

everything: a partner's changes, your discoveries

packed into crates and stowed

in a rented unit. I'm telling you,

do it if you want, don't do it if you don't;

stigma, while still there, is less, so much less

and it's a big, big world. Your friends become

family. Find a good traveling buddy. Fall in love;

if it's good, stay. If not, leave.

I hope I don't sound glib, we just have more options

now and for that, for you, I'm glad.

Mamma Bear

Bears: If it's brown, lay down; if it's black, attack;
if it's white, goodnight.

I
It's Mother's day. We are,
my grown daughter and I
in the clouding-over yard,
playing with bows and arrows
two bottles of prosecco in our guts
velocity and barbs lethal in our woman hands;
the rage the rage of all things female rises.
I am ready, arrow nocked, rage
of my sisters my cells afire mitochondrial DNA
boils and tighter twists I see,
losing my mind a little,
a man's image on the target,
release the spear, point through throat.

II
I have been told no so often
it has lost all meaning for me.
I have taken, grabbed when I needed to
grabbed. I
will not be denied myself.

I, PhD, worked full time and wrote.
I, author, write books.
I, executive, guide organizations.
I, glassblower, create art.
I, strategist, took down a congressman.
I, mother, grandmother, am the white bear.

I am blue in the brain,
and the red blood, the blood has fled
my shriveled uterus.
I am tired, I am tired
having to grab and fight the same fight
of being a body a body a body.

I am tired of telling
I am done with this.
I can see it, I have seen it, held the hands of,
spoken with women, I know them, the violated,
there on the sand, on the sand,
I see it, it's coming.

Your religion, my god,
we are lost under the tree, lost in the dark woods.
I am furious. I am the sand.

I am the wind. I am the fire.
I am the blood. I am the body.

I will not be silent, my life
has been a story of fearlessness,
my name is in the book
I walk the dunes, the wadis
the dry riverbeds, the stones, the sand
I will now tell you, I will tell you and not
I am not willing to listen, will not listen,
we are done. I am the fire. The sand.
The body, the blood, the brain.
I am the white bear.   I am not afraid.

Mermaid

She fell over, over the side of the boat's rail in her coat,
dress, her chemise, the petticoats, shoes, whalebone
corset returning to the sea, their waterlogged bulk
         pulled her below.

Night and cold, no one saw her go.
Arms akimbo,
a push at the salt air abandoning her pink lungs at last
when the whale, not a baleen feeder with gaping mouth, or
orca with sharpened teeth, or narwhal with spiraled tusk,

no,

a sperm whale opened its narrow jaw,
took her in,
closed the hinge.

She was *delicious;*

he rolled her over his tongue, around, pressed her against

the bony palate, a sweet change from giant squid deep
down, those fighters with hooked tentacles tearing his skin:

Is that what I have to do for a meal,
said in pings and squeaks, whale-speak,
when this tidbit, although better without the wool—and
pointy shoes—might slide so easily into my stomach?

He took a tooth (however a whale might do such a
thing), laid it atop her chest and pressed,
skin broke, ivory softened, soaked the still heart,
     one beat,   a second;
legs fused, slips fell away; gill-slits above breasts
bloomed; corneas curved.

He spat her out.

She woke without a gasp,
all that fish know swimming, swimming in her.
She, transformed to fill the seas with easy meals.

No.

She, to a wreck below dived, forged rusted iron cannons into harpoons, tridents, with each hammer strike her siren voice singing:

No one, no one is going to eat **my** *young.*

Vixen

It's the fur they see first; not foxes, humans—coveting
our jaw-dropping red-brown luster in sunlight.

I often feel a cobbled-together beast, pool or puddle
reflects raccoon, corgi, coyote depending on the light,
the angle, mouth open or closed;

now I'll tell you (without kindness) we're not sly or
cunning, that's your mistake; it's intelligence
and hard work, if at first you don't succeed and all that.

You've been told.

About the Author

Lori Heninger is a poet and nonprofit executive. Her 30-plus years of experience in US- and internationally-based work has shaped her thinking and writing. She is the author of poems published in The *Bangalore Review*, *The Dillydoun Review* and other journals, as well as *Managing As Mission: Nonprofit Managing for Sustainable Change,* and a book of poetry for children titled *Outside/Inside/Outside*. Lori graduated from Columbia University with a Masters in Social Work and from City University with a PhD in Social Welfare. She is the Executive Director of The Montclair Fund for Women, and lives with her husband, two dogs, a cat and six chickens in rural New Jersey, and blows glass as a hobby.

Acknowledgements

This chapbook would not exist without Project Write Now in Red Bank, NJ, and instructor, mentor and friend, Laura Cyphers. Laura's expertise and positive, kind critique style allowed me the spaciousness to feel like my writing mattered. I can't thank her enough.

My early readers, Lou Storey and Gay Norton Edelman, provided invaluable input and encouragement, and Jen Burger provided much-needed moral support.

Thank you to Stephanie Lamb and the team at Quillkeepers Press for being excited about and publishing these poems.

Finally, thank you to my family: Marc, Thea and Aidan. I love you all more than I can write.